Frog or Toad?

How Do You Know?

WHICH ANIMAL ? IS WHICH?

Melissa Stewart

Enslow Elementary

an imprint of

E **Enslow Publishers, Inc.**
40 Industrial Road
Box 398
Berkeley Heights, NJ 07922
USA

http://www.enslow.com

Contents

Words to Know 3

Do You Know? 4

Wet or Dry? 6

Long or Short Legs? 8

Thin or Fat? 10

Teeth or No Teeth? 12

Loud or Quiet? 14

Clumps or Chains? 16

Now Do You Know? 18

What a Surprise! 20

Learn More:

   Books 22

   Web Sites 23

Index 24

Words to Know

jaw (JAW)—One of the two bones that make an animal's mouth. Teeth grow out of the jaw.

moist (MOYST)—A little bit wet.

predator (PREH duh tur)—An animal that hunts and kills other animals for food.

prey (PRAY)—An animal that is hunted by a predator.

tadpole (TAD pohl)—A young frog, toad, or salamander.

Do You Know?

Which of these animals is a frog? Which one is a toad? Do you know?

Wet or Dry?

Marsh frog

A frog has wet, slimy skin. It needs to live close to water.

A toad has drier, bumpy skin. The skin keeps water inside the toad's body. That is why toads can live farther from water than frogs.

European toad

Long or Short Legs?

European tree frog

A frog has long, strong back legs. They are perfect for jumping and swimming.

A toad has short back legs. Toads walk or take small hops.

American toad

Thin or Fat?

A frog has a long, thin body. This shape helps a frog make long leaps to get away from predators.

Green tree frog

Southern toad

A toad has a fat, round body. Its skin smells and tastes bad, so predators leave it alone.

Teeth or No Teeth?

Tree frog

A frog has teeth on its upper **jaw**. There are no teeth on a frog's lower jaw. Frogs use their teeth to hold **prey**.

A toad does not have teeth. It must swallow prey quickly.

European toad

Loud or Quiet?

A male frog sings loudly on warm spring nights. A female frog follows the sound to find the male. Then the frogs mate.

African giant bullfrog

American toad

A male toad sings quietly for just a few minutes. Then he stops for a while. But a female toad can still find him.

Clumps or Chains?

A female frog lays eggs in clumps. A thick, slippery coating keeps them **moist** until they hatch.

A female toad lays eggs in long chains. After a few days, the eggs hatch and tiny **tadpoles** swim out.

Now Do You Know?

This animal has teeth in its upper jaw.

It sings loudly to attract a mate.

Its body is long and thin.

It lays eggs in clumps.

Green frog

It has wet, slimy skin.

It has long back legs.

It's a frog!

18

This animal has no teeth.

It sings quietly to attract a mate.

Its body is fat and round.

It lays eggs in long chains.

Cane toad

It has dry, bumpy skin.

It has short legs.

It's a toad!

What a Surprise!

Almost five thousand kinds of frogs live on Earth today.

Poison dart frog

Tree frog

Harlequin poison dart frog

Ornate horned frog

About five hundred kinds of these frogs are "true toads." They are what you picture when someone says the word "toad."

Bumpy toad

Black toad

American toad

Green toad

That means all toads are frogs, but not all frogs are toads.

Learn More

Books

Bishop, Nic. Frogs. New York, Scholastic, 2008.

Carney, Elizabeth. Frogs! Washington, D.C.: National Geographic, 2009.

French, Vivian. Growing Frogs. New York: Walker Books, 2008.

Moffet, Mark. Face to Face with Frogs. Washington, D.C.: National Geographic, 2010.

Stewart, Melissa. A Place for Frogs. Atlanta, Ga.: Peachtree Publishers, 2010.

Web Sites

All About Frogs for Kids and Teachers.
http://www.kiddyhouse.com/Themes/frogs

Frogs: A Chorus of Colors.
http://www.amnh.org/exhibitions/frogs

Frog and Toad Videos.
http://video.nationalgeographic.com/video/
player/animals/amphibians-animals/
frogs-and-toads
Click on "Animals
Video," "Amphibians,"
then "Frogs and Toads."

Index

body, 10, 11, 18, 19

eggs, 16, 17, 18, 19

jaw, 12

jump, 8

legs, 8, 9, 18, 19

predator, 10–11

prey, 12, 13

skin, 6, 7, 11, 18, 19

sound, 14, 15, 18, 19

tadpoles, 17

teeth, 12, 13, 18, 19

walk, 9

water, 6, 7

24

Enslow Elementary, an imprint of Enslow Publishers, Inc.
Enslow Elementary® is a registered trademark of Enslow Publishers, Inc.

Copyright © 2011 by Melissa Stewart

Library of Congress Cataloging-in-Publication Data

Stewart, Melissa
    Frog or toad? : how do you know? / Melissa Stewart.
        p. cm. — (Which animal is which?)
    Includes bibliographical references and index.
    Summary: "Explains to young readers how to tell the difference between frogs and toads"—
        Provided by publisher.
    Library Ed. ISBN 978-0-7660-3682-6
    Paperback ISBN 978-1-59845-236-5
    1. Frogs—Juvenile literature. 2. Toads—Juvenile literature. I. Title.
    QL668.E2S743 2011
    597.8—dc22   2010003277

Printed in the United States of America
102010 Lake Book Manufacturing, Inc., Melrose Park, IL

10 9 8 7 6 5 4 3 2 1

To Our Readers: We have done our best to make sure all Internet Addresses in this book were active and appropriate when we went to press. However, the author and the publisher have no control over and assume no liability for the material available on those Internet sites or on other Web sites they may link to. Any comments or suggestions can be sent by e-mail to comments@ enslow.com or to the address on the back cover.

♻ Enslow Publishers, Inc., is committed to printing our books on recycled paper. The paper in every book contains 10% to 30% post-consumer waste (PCW). The cover board on the outside of each book contains 100% PCW. Our goal is to do our part to help young people and the environment too!

Note to Parents and Teachers: The *Which Animal Is Which?* series supports the National Science Education Standards for K–4 science. The Words to Know section introduces subject-specific vocabulary words, including pronunciation and definitions. Early readers may need help with these new words.

Photo Credits: imagebroker.net/Photolibrary, p. 15; Millard H. Sharp/Photo Researchers, Inc., p. 9; Minden Pictures: © Fabio Liverani/NPL, p. 12, © Hugo Wilcox/Foto Natura, p. 6, © Jose B. Ruiz, p. 7, © Jose Luis Gomez de Francisco/NPL, p. 17, © Kim Taylor/NPL, pp. 2, 13, © Piotr Naskrecki, p. 21 (Central coast stubfoot toad), © Stephen Dalton, pp. 3, 8, © Thomas Marent, pp. 1 (toad), 5, 19; Peter Arnold Images/Photolibrary, p. 11, Shutterstock.com, pp. 1 (frog), 4, 10, 14, 16, 18, 20, 21, 23.

Cover Photos: Shutterstock.com (left), © Thomas Marent/Minden Pictures (right).